ICE AGES

ICE AGES
WHEN THE WORLD CHILLS OUT

RUSSELL FERRETT

young
reed

First published in Australia in 2010 by Young Reed, an imprint of
New Holland Publishers (Australia) Pty Ltd
Sydney • Auckland • London • Cape Town

www.youngreed.com.au

1/66 Gibbes Street Chatswood NSW 2067 Australia
218 Lake Road Northcote Auckland New Zealand
86 Edgware Road London W2 2EA United Kingdom
80 McKenzie Street Cape Town 8001 South Africa

National Library of Australia Cataloguing-in-Publication Data:

Ferrett, Russell Richard.
Ice ages / Russ Ferrett.
1st ed.
SBN: 9781921073564 (hbk.)
Series: Young reed.
Includes index.
Bibliography.

For primary school age.

Glacial epoch—Juvenile literature.

551.792

Publisher: Fiona Schultz
Publishing manager: Lliane Clarke
Designer: Emma Gough
Project editor: Rochelle Fernandez
Production manager: Olga Dementiev
Printer: Toppan Leefung Printing Limited

CONTENTS

WHAT IF WE HAVE A NEW ICE AGE?

The last ice age finished around 12,000 years ago. In the past, ice ages have often followed periods of global warming. What do you think it would be like if we had another ice age right now? What would it be like at your home? Would it be too cold? If it was, where would you like to move to?

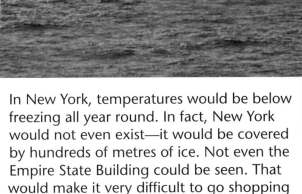

NEW YORK, USA
At present,
normal daily temperature range in January
-4° to 3°C (25° to 37° F)
normal daily temperature range in July
19° to 28° C (66° to 82° F)

In New York, temperatures would be below freezing all year round. In fact, New York would not even exist—it would be covered by hundreds of metres of ice. Not even the Empire State Building could be seen. That would make it very difficult to go shopping on Fifth Avenue, wouldn't it?

MOSCOW, RUSSIA

At present,
normal daily temperature range in January -16° to -9°C
(3°to16°F)
normal daily temperature range in July
13° to 3°C (55° to 73°F)

While Moscow would be as cold as New York, it wouldn't be covered by a glacier. That's because too little snow would fall. It would be a frozen desert. Would you want to live in a place where mid-summer temperatures rise above 0°C (32°F) for only a few weeks of the year?

LONDON, GREAT BRITAIN

Normal daily temperature range in
January 2° to 6°C (36° to 43°F)
Normal daily temperature range in July
14° to 22°C (57° to 72°F)

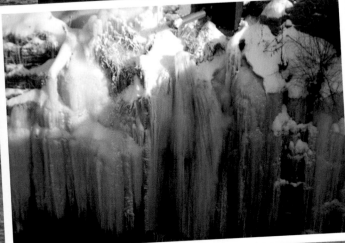

Winter temperatures in London would stay below 0°C (32°F) for months and July temperatures would be much cooler than at present, seldom rising above 10°C (50°F). While most of the snow would melt in summer, the ground would be so wet and soggy all the trees would die. You wouldn't want to live here—only 200 or 300 kilometres (125 to 185 miles) north of the city, a huge glacier would cover the landscape.

At present, normal daily temperature range in January –14°–1°C (7°–33°F) normal daily temperature range in July 7°–27°C (45°– 81°F)

If a new ice age forced you to migrate, you could safely choose to move to the tropics or the continents of Africa, Australia and South America. All these locations would be a little cooler, but they'd still be great places in which to live.

In Colorado, glaciers more than 150 metres (500 feet) deep would fill the valleys and snow would cover the lower slopes for at least nine months of the year. The tree line would be much lower than at present and permanent snow would cover the peaks. The aspen trees that give the town its name would have all disappeared and been replaced by conifers. It would still be a great place to go skiing though—especially in summer when you could ski on the glaciers.

SINGAPORE
At present,
normal daily temperature range in January
23° to 30°C (73° to 86°F)
normal daily temperature range in July
24° to 31°C (75° to 88°F)

If you visited Singapore today you would find it to be very hot and steamy. Likewise, if you visited during an ice age, the weather would not have changed much. At just a few degrees cooler, temperatures each day, all year round, would average 19° to 27°C (66° to 81°F). Sounds great—but it would be very crowded. Everyone would want to come here for their holidays.

SYDNEY, AUSTRALIA
At present,
normal daily temperature range in January
18°–26°C (64°–79°F)
normal daily temperature range in July
8°–16°C (46°–61°F)

During a new ice age, Sydney would change from a city with hot summers and cool sunny winters to one with warm summers and colder winters. It still wouldn't be cold enough to snow though and would be a very pleasant place to live. If you wanted to go skiing, you'd have to head west of the city to the Blue Mountains.

WHEN THE EARTH GETS COLD

IN NORTH AMERICA

Most of Canada and the northern part of the lower 48 states of America were covered by permanent ice and snow for thousands and thousands of years. Canada was joined to Greenland, but large parts of Alaska remained ice-free. Dry land also existed between Alaska and Russia. Glaciers in the Rocky Mountains and Cascade Ranges in the west of the continent were of the valley type similar to those found in Europe's Alps.

During the ice ages, these mountains in Peru would have been covered with snow rather than by trees as we see them now. In the higher mountains where snow is found today, the snow would have been much deeper and fallen much further down the slopes. Snow showers would have started early in autumn and continued well into summer.

HOW COLD DID IT GET?

During the last ice age, worldwide temperatures were 4° to 8°C (7° to 14°F) below those of today. At these lower temperatures some European countries such as Norway, Sweden, Finland, Estonia, Latvia, Lithuania, Denmark, Holland, and Iceland were completely covered by ice and snow all year round. Others such as Great Britain, Ireland, Belgium, Germany, Poland and Russia were only partly covered.

WHY DID IT SUDDENLY BECOME COLDER?

Scientists don't know exactly why the earth's climate sometimes cools down. Some think it is because, like a fire, the sun is hotter at some times and cooler at other times before heating up again. Other scientists think it may be caused by a combination of small movements in the earth's orbit and changes in the tilt of the earth's axis. Still others believe it could be caused by a lowering of the amount of greenhouse gases in the atmosphere. Perhaps it is a combination of all these factors?

ANOTHER THEORY

Ireland's lush green grass depends on the warmth of the Gulf Stream. All of Western Europe and Scandinavia lie much closer to the North Pole than does New York, yet places like London have much warmer winters than New York. The warm Gulf Stream flows north from Florida, across the Atlantic and along the west coast of Europe. If this ocean current were to stop flowing, Western Europe would become very much colder.

THE LAST ICE AGE

The last ice age, however, was not the first. In fact, the earth has had many ice ages in the past. The last series of ice ages started around two million years ago in a geological period called the Pleistocene. At the start of the Pleistocene, temperatures gradually cooled and large areas of the world became covered by ice. Then, after thousands of years, temperatures gradually rose to much the same as today. They remained warm for thousands of years before gradually becoming cold again and the ice covering returned.

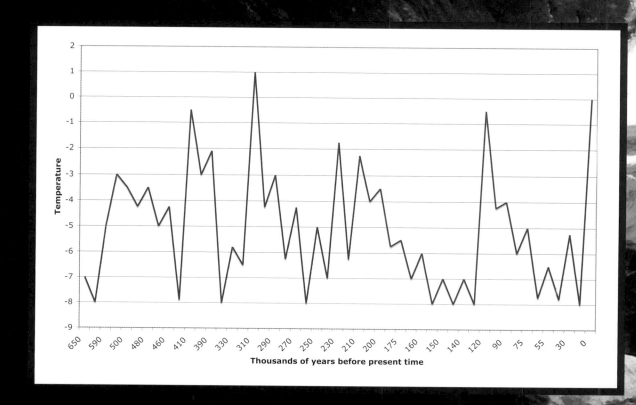

THE ICE AGES COULDN'T MAKE UP THEIR MIND

This pattern of hot—cold—hot—cold—hot... has been repeated many times. The cold periods are referred to as 'glacials' or 'stages' of the ice age, and the warmer periods as 'inter-glacials'. Even during each cold stage and each of the inter-glacial period, temperatures constantly change, sometimes getting a little warmer and at other times getting a little colder.

SNOWBALL EARTH

Not all ice ages are the same—some have even been much colder than any experienced in the Pleistocene. The coldest was around 600 to 700 million years ago, long before humans existed and even before the time of the dinosaurs. This ice age was so cold that the surface of most oceans, including those near the equator, froze. Scientists estimate that temperatures would have been more than 25°C (45°F) colder than at present and refer to this time as 'Snowball Earth'. Why do you think they use this name?

DOWNTOWN GLACIERS

Hallett Cove, just south of Adelaide in Australia, is an area where scientists have discovered ancient rocks that were scoured by glaciers 280 million years ago. That's a long time before the last series of ice ages, but still not as old as Snowball Earth.

ICE, ICE AND MORE ICE

Do you know there are some places on earth still in an ice age? It is so cold in Antarctica and central Greenland that they are still covered by ice all year round. These places are very cold because they lie near the Earth's Poles.

A 'COOL' PLACE TO VISIT

The coldest temperature ever recorded on earth since the invention of thermometers is –89°C (–129°F) at a scientific station in Antarctica. Can you imagine how cold that is? If you threw a bucket of water out the window, the water would freeze solid before it hit the ground—and it was even colder there during the ice ages.

WHY IS IT SO COLD NEAR THE POLES?

The Earth's polar areas are cold for three main reasons:

1. Unlike in the tropics, the sun never shines directly down on them. Even in the middle of summer, the sun never gets to be very high in the sky. This means, its rays have to pass through a greater distance of atmosphere before they reach the ground and so have lost a lot of heat before reaching the earth's surface here.

2. When the sun's rays reach the earth they strike it at a low angle and are easily reflected back into space. Reflection is further aided by the shiny nature of the water and ice found on the earth's surface near the poles.

3. Each bundle of rays has to heat up more land surface near the poles than it has to near the tropics. If you look at the diagram, you can see that the sun's rays heat a much smaller section of the earth than a similar sized bundle of rays striking the earth near the poles.

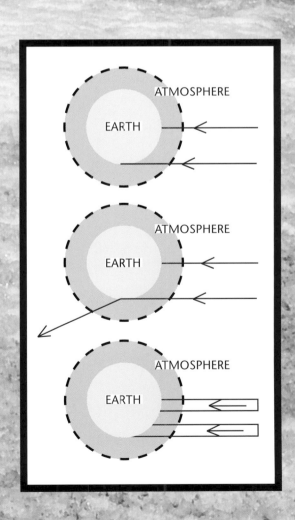

HOW ICY IS THE WORLD?

Almost 90 per cent of the world's glacial ice is located in Antarctica and nearly 10 per cent in Greenland. That leaves less than 1 per cent of the world's glacial ice to be found elsewhere. There is so much ice in glaciers worldwide that if it were all placed on the lower 48 states of America, or Australia, it would cover it to a depth of nearly 4 kilometres (2½ miles). Not even the Rocky Mountains or the Great Dividing Range would peek out above the ice.

IT WAS ICIER STILL

During the last ice age there was enough ice to cover the main part of America (or Australia) to a depth of 11 kilometres (7 miles). At that time Antarctica didn't have much more ice than it has now, but Europe and North America each had extremely large glaciers nearly the same size as the one in Antarctica.

WHAT IF IT ALL MELTS?

If all the world's present glaciers melted, the worldwide sea level would rise by around 65 metres (215 feet). Countries like Bangladesh, Holland and island nations in the Pacific would be completely covered by the ocean. Great sections of Russia, the USA and Europe would be drowned and many coastal cities such as London, New York, Tokyo and Shanghai would be flooded.

FROM THIS

TO THIS

WHERE DID SNOW AND ICE COME FROM?

SEA LEVELS DROP

It's a bit like starting with a full bucket of water. If you take a full cup out and then put half a cup back, and you repeat this over and over, what happens to the level of water in the bucket? It goes down. That's what happens to the oceans during an ice age. More water is taken out of the oceans by evaporation than runs back into them and it causes sea levels to fall. During the cold stages of an ice age, worldwide sea levels fell around 130 metres (425 feet).

LIKE TO CANOE THE EVERGLADES?

It would be great, wouldn't it? But not during the ice ages. The fall in sea level resulted in all coastlines being much further out to sea than they are at present. Florida was twice as large as it is today. All the sea floor that is now covered by water less than 130 metres (425 feet) deep became dry land. The Florida Everglades would have been well above sea level and its swamps would have drained into the ocean, leaving you and your canoe stranded on dry land.

You know about the water cycle, don't you? It's how rain, hail and snow falls from clouds to the ground. The snow and hail melt and join with rainwater to flow into rivers. The rivers then flow into the sea. Water evaporates into the atmosphere where it forms clouds and from these clouds we get more rain, hail and snow. The cycle goes on and on, over and over. That's why it's called a cycle—it goes round and round forever.

AN INTERRUPTED CYCLE

During an ice age, the water cycle gets a puncture! Not all of the water runs back into the sea. Instead, snow that falls in very cold places remains frozen on the ground. This snow builds up year after year, becoming deeper and deeper to the point where the bottom layers become compressed and turn into ice.

HOW DO GLACIERS FORM AND GROW?

Glaciers start as big piles of snow. If more snow falls in winter than melts in summer the snow becomes deeper every year. For example, if 5 metres of snow falls in winter and only 4 melts in summer, there'll be 1 metre of snow left on the ground at the beginning of next winter. If the next winter another 5 metres fall, there'll be 6 metres on the ground. If only 4 metres of snow melt over that summer, there'll be 2 metres of snow at the start of the next winter. Each year the snow gets 1 metre deeper than the previous year—over hundreds of years, the snow will become hundreds of metres deep.

YOU NEED LOTS OF SNOW TO MAKE A GLACIER

The snow here is 5 metres (16 feet) deep, but it's not all the same. Snow at the top is light and fluffy, but at the bottom it's compressed and on its way to becoming ice.

SNOW IS SOFT, BUT ICE IS HARD

Snow is made of 10 per cent ice and 90 per cent air. That's why snow is so soft. If you have a deep pile of snow, the top layers are heavy enough to squeeze the air out of the bottom layers, making them more like ice than snow. In addition, during summer, water from the melting top layers seeps down to the bottom layers where it fills the air spaces and refreezes. In just a few years 1 metre (3 feet) of snow will be compressed to become 10 centimetres (4 inches) of solid ice.

FROM SNOW TO ICE

If you go to the snow in winter you can see how compression works. When you walk in the snow you leave deep footprints. Your feet compress the snow and turn it into ice. If you make a snowman, you pack the snow with your hands as you build. The packing partly turns the snow to ice and makes your snowman stronger. If you make a snowball to throw at a friend, you compress the snow in your hands before you throw the snowball so that it will hold together until it hits your target. But don't squeeze too hard—you wouldn't want to hit anyone with an ice ball, would you?

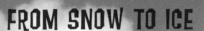

TWO TYPES OF GLACIERS

Glacial ice is the same; it's just compressed snow. However, not all glaciers are the same. Large glaciers that cover whole continents or mountain tops and fill valleys are termed 'continental glaciers'. Smaller glaciers, those usually found high up in mountains, are called 'valley' or 'alpine' glaciers and are like rivers of ice.

GLACIAL MOVEMENT

Have you ever been accused of being 'as slow as a wet week'? Well, now that you know a little about glaciers, you could tell someone they are 'as slow as a glacier'. A wet week may seem to take a long time to pass, but a glacier moves even slower. A continental glacier may move at less than 100 metres (330 feet) a year while a really speedy valley glacier can move at 5 metres (16 feet) a day.

This one's on a slippery side. Here, a valley glacier simply slides down its valley. The steeper the valley floor, the faster it moves.

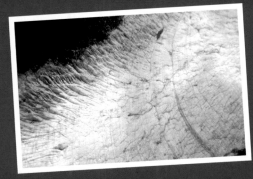

A SOLID THAT CAN FLOW

Looking down on a valley glacier, you'll see crescent-shaped lines running across it from one side to the other. These crescents always point downstream. The original lines run straight across, but as a glacier slides down the valley, its centre travels faster than the edges. The edges are slowed down as they get caught against the valley sides while the centre keeps moving at a more constant rate. That's just like a straight running river isn't it? Water flows fastest in the centre of a stream and slowest along its edges.

AND TURN CORNERS

When a valley glacier goes around a corner it continues to act like a river. The fastest movement then takes place along the outside of the bend while movement on the inside of the bend slows down. Crevasses may develop in a glacier's surface on the outside of bends.

CREVASSES ARE CRACKS

If a valley glacier passes over a hump in the rock over which it is flowing or turns a bend, it will develop cracks in its upper surface. These cracks—or crevasses—extend down into the solid ice below. Crevasses are never deeper than 100 metres (330 feet). If they went any deeper, pressure from the ice above would force the bottom of the crevasse to close. It's like trying to dig a hole in a tub of thick yoghurt. As you dig the hole, pressure from the top forces the hole to close.

THE BIG PANCAKE

Continental glaciers are so big that they're not affected by hills and valleys—they just flow right over the top of them. They move by extrusion, which is the type of movement you get when you pour a thick pancake mix into a pan. If you keep pouring onto the same spot, the mixture piles up, but then spreads out in all directions from the centre. If you have heavy snow falls in the centre of a glacier it pushes down and forces the ice at the bottom to spread out.

WHAT ABOUT THE HILLS?

Most continental glaciers are over a kilometre thick. If a hill is not as high as the glacier is thick, the glacier will flow over it. Likewise, if a mountain is higher than the glacier is thick, the glacier will flow around it. Such mountains, like those in Antarctica and Greenland, poke up through the glacier and look like islands in a sea of ice.

ANTARCTICA: STUCK IN AN ICE AGE

During the ice ages, as we've seen, northern parts of both Europe and North America were covered by ice in the same way that Antarctica is covered today. For this reason scientists go to the continent to study its climate and its glaciers. Perhaps one day you would like to be an Antarctic scientist?

MORE PEOPLE LIVE HERE THAN YOU THINK

In summer, Antartica's population swells to around 4000 people, but it drops in winter. Antarctica has no permanent inhabitants and most people stay for less than 15 months. There are more than 40 scientific bases on or close to the continent. Most bases are small with populations of around 50 in summer and 15–20 in winter. The largest base, McMurdo, is run by Americans and has a summer population of around 1000 and a winter population of 250.

SPRING-CLEANING IN THE ANTARCTIC?

These scientists look as if they are doing a spring clean-up, but they're not. They're sweeping and collecting snow. Until temperatures rise high enough to melt the snow in summer, the scientists' only supply of water at this small base comes from gathering snow and melting it in the warm interior of their huts.

THE ICE

Ice has covered Antarctica for millions of years. It has not melted even during the warmest of interglacials. Permanent ice covers 99.7 per cent of the continent. The ice has an average thickness of nearly 2 kilometres (6500 feet), but at its deepest is nearly 5 kilometres (16 400 feet) thick.

ICE SHELVES

Floating sea ice permanently covers Antarctica's two huge bays and many other smaller bays around its coast. The largest of the ice shelves is 1½ times the size of Germany. Sea ice is frozen ocean water, but is not salty. As sea water freezes, the salt is squeezed out into the unfrozen water beneath the ice. Weddell seals live and hunt under the thin edges of the floating ice by keeping breathing holes open during the winter. The ice shelves are vulnerable to warming temperatures and some are breaking up as a result of global warming.

BIRDS AND ANIMALS

The sea is the only food source for Antarctic wildlife. As such, animal life is dominated by swimmers—be they fish, whales, seals or birds. Most birds migrate to the continent in summer and leave in winter. Only penguins stay all year round and then only to use the land surface for standing on and raising their chicks; the ice and frozen ground provides them with no food.

OVERWEIGHT?
BEEN EATING THE WRONG FOOD?

Elephant seals live around the edge of Antarctica and its ice shelves. The animals can grow to over 5 metres (16 feet) long and can weigh more than two tonnes. Much of their weight is fat. Unlike humans for whom excess fat is unhealthy, elephant seals in these freezing waters require layers of fat to keep them warm. Seal and humans are both mammals and so are warm blooded.

THE HIGHEST AND LOWEST POINTS

The highest mountain in Antarctica is Mt Vinson. It rises 4892 metres (16,050 feet) above sea level and stands out above the ice. The thickest covering of ice is not found near the highest mountain, but above a depression in the continent where the solid rock beneath the ice sheet lies 2500 metres (8200 feet) below sea level.

SHAPING THE ROCK BENEATH THE ICE

IT'S NOT A BULLDOZER

As a glacier moves over the surface, it doesn't push large mounds of soil and rock in front of it like a bulldozer. Rather, the glacier moves over the top of the surface. The sandy and rocky material it passes over gets caught under the ice and is carried along with the glacier as it moves forward.

IT'S A RASP

Ice on its own is not a very good cutting tool—have you ever tried sharpening a pencil with an ice cube? But with all that sand and rock wedged in the bottom of the ice, the glacier is turned into a giant rasp. Although the rasping glacier moves very slowly, it has millions of tonnes of ice pushing down on it and millions and millions of teeth. In this way the glacier becomes a much more effective eroder of the land surface than either running water or the wind. A small valley glacier can move more rock in 50 thousand years than a river can in 5 million years.

WHICH DIRECTION?

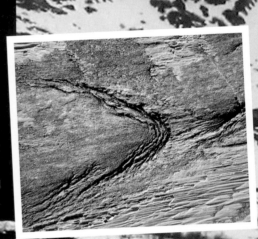

If you were standing where this photo was taken, you'd know that the glacier was moving from right to left. But as you're not there, you'll have to look for clues. Did you see the first one? The scratches run from right to left. There's another clue—see the big 'V' in the centre of the photo? These 'V's are called 'chatter marks'. Chatter marks are made in solid rock by the glacier as it plucks out small pieces of gravel that get caught beneath the ice. Chatter marks always point in the direction from which the ice came. Here, it points to the right, proving this glacier was moving from right to left.

BIG ROCKS

Continental glaciers are capable of moving very large rocks and carrying them long distances. This large sandstone block is 8 metres (25 feet) long, 5 metres (16 feet) wide and 5 metres high. It weighs over 300 tonnes and was plucked from the side of a hill and carried about 3 kilometres (2 miles). We know this because the rock is of a different type to the rock underneath. Rocks carried in this way are called 'erratics'.

BIG ROCKS DON'T LAST LONG UNDER THE ICE

The big erratic above would have become much smaller if it had been carried for a greater distance. As the ice carried it along it would have been worn away by its contact with the solid rock under the glacier. So in wearing away the solid rock below, it was also wearing away itself. These erratics would have been much larger when they were first picked up by the glacier and carried a greater distance before the glacier melted.

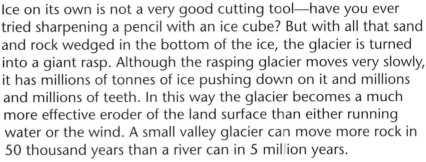

IT'S GONE TOO FAR. RETREAT! RETREAT!

RETREAT! RETREAT!
20 − 30 = ?
So what is needed for the glacial snout to move backwards? If the glacier moves forward 20 metres/yards in the year, but the snout melts back by 30 metres/yards, the glacier's snout will retreat by 10 metres/yards. This is what happens during global warming and is why many of the world's alpine glaciers are retreating.

ADVANCING GLACIERS
10 + 10 − 6 = ?
Glaciers move further in winter than in summer. That's because it's usually cold enough in winter for the glacier's snout to remain frozen. If a glacier slides forward 10 metres/yards in winter, it will probably slide another 10 metres/yards forward in summer. However, if 6 metres/yards melts off the snout of the glacier in summer, it will have moved forward only 4 metres/yards. Under these conditions, the snout will have moved forward a total of 14 metres/yards and the glacier is said to be 'advancing'.

IN BALANCE OR EQUILIBRIUM
10 + 10 − 20 = ?
If the same glacier was to slide forward 10 metres/yards in winter and a further 10 metres/yards in summer, but 20 metres/yards melted off the snout in summer, the snout of the glacier would remain stationery from year to year. The glacier would then be in balance or equilibrium, where the speed of melting is equal to the speed of forward movement.

26

Glaciers move forward as they receive more and more snow. But what happens if the snow stops falling or temperatures increase? They get smaller; they retreat. But retreating doesn't mean they begin to slide back uphill—that's impossible. Gravity won't allow that. Can you sit at the bottom of a slippery slide and hope to slide back to the top? A glacier cannot slide back up a mountain valley.

ADVANCE AND RETREAT OF CONTINENTAL GLACIERS

As valley glaciers can't slide back uphill, it's also impossible for continental glaciers covering the whole landscape to slide backwards. The maths is the same for them as for the smaller valley glaciers. As more snow falls in the centre of a continental glacier, the increased pressure pushes the edges outwards and the glacier advances. If less snow falls, there is less pressure at the centre and less outward push to the edges.

EQUILIBRIUM AND RETREAT

If the outward movement of a continental glacier is equalled by the rate of backward melting, the snout will be in equilibrium. If temperatures rise and the rate of melting increases, the ice will keep moving forward, but the snout will retreat and the glacier will become smaller. At the end of the last stage of the last ice age, the temperatures in northern Canada increased by 8°C (13°F) over a period of around 5000 years. Over that time the North America continental glacier retreated more than 2000 kilometres (1250 miles) and went from an area greater than 10 million square kilometres (3,860,000 square miles) to nothing.

REARRANGING THE RIVERS

BEFORE THE GLACIER

Before the ice ages, many North American rivers followed different paths to the sea than they do today. The Missouri River flowed north through Canada to Hudson Bay and the Ohio River didn't even exist. Another river that no longer exists, The Teays, followed a path north of the present day Ohio, to join the Mississippi. We do not know the exact paths of these rivers as the scouring action of glaciers during the ice ages removed much of the evidence of their existence. Lake Superior was the only one of the Great Lakes to exist before the ice ages.

THEN CAME THE ICE

The heaviest snowfalls occurred around Newfoundland and Hudson Bay and created the great North American glacier. As the glacier grew, its first victim was the north-flowing Missouri. A kilometre high wall of ice blocked the river forming Lake Agassiz, a lake larger than all the present-day Great Lakes combined. The lake eventually overflowed and cut a new path for the Missouri to join the Mississippi and flow south. As the glacier expanded it next blocked the mouth of the St Lawrence River, forcing the waters of the Great Lakes region to flow south down the Hudson River or west to the Mississippi.

RELENTLESS ICE

As the ice moved south it eventually covered all the St Lawrence Valley, the ancient Teays River and scoured out the Great Lakes. The Ohio River formed along the south-eastern front of the glacier to drain away the huge quantities of water that flowed from the melting glacier. The new Missouri performed the same task along the south-western front.

THEN IT STARTED TO MELT ...

As the glacier melted, the old Teays River filled with sand and rock allowing the Ohio to continue to flow. The Great Lakes filled with melt-water and the St Lawrence River reappeared as the ice retreated.

NIAGARA FALLS WAS BORN

The Niagara River, which is really an extension of the St Lawrence, flowed out of Lake Erie into Lake Ontario. As the surface of Lake Erie is 51 metres (167 feet) above that of Lake Ontario, the Niagara River has to drop by that amount, and in so doing, formed Niagara Falls.
The Detroit and Sarnia Rivers in a similar manner flowed from Lake Huron into Lake Erie and the St Marys River flowed from Lake Superior into lake Huron.

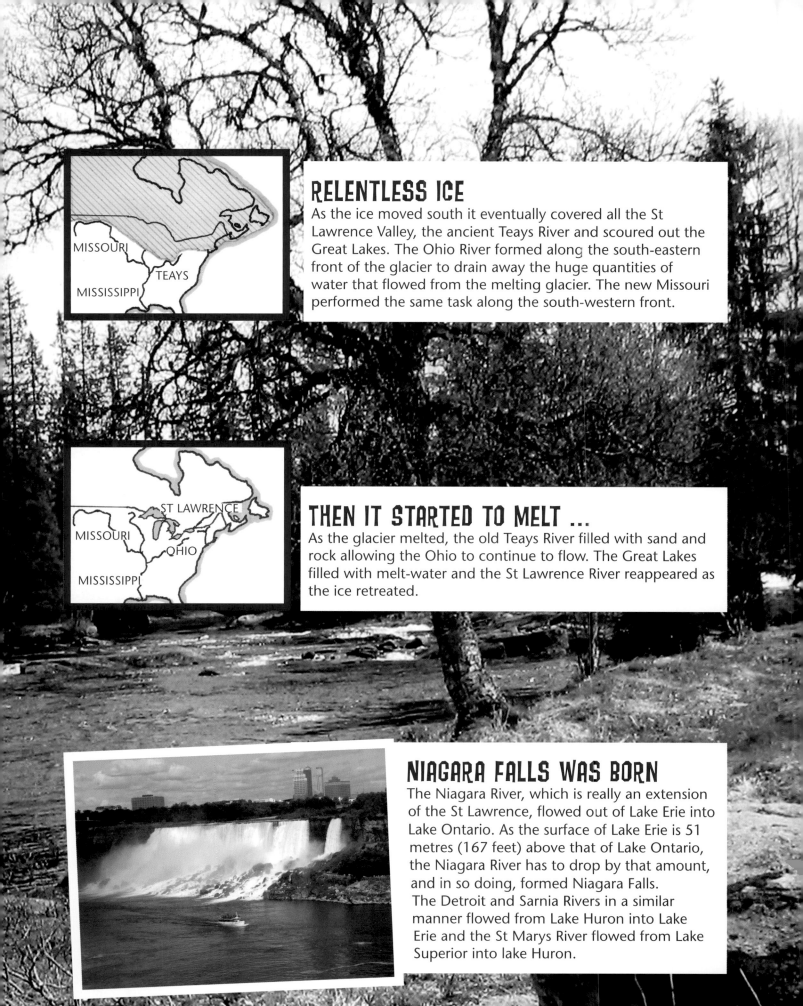

AFTER THE GLACIERS HAVE GONE

As the ice disappeared, fresh surfaces were exposed that were quite different to those existing prior to the ice age. In the areas under the centres of continental glaciers, large scour plains dotted with lakes were created. After hundreds of thousands of years of rasping by the glacial ice, the tops of the hills were rounded and smoothed off.

DISAPPEARING ROCK

In North America, the rock gouged out of Canada was carried south by the glacier into the USA. When the glacier stopped advancing, the sand and gravel carried beneath the ice was dropped in huge mounds at the glacier's snout. These mounds, called moraines, were then eroded into rolling hills by the melt-water flowing from the glacier.

RETREATING ICE

As temperatures rose, the ice kept moving forward but the snout melted back even faster. As it melted, the glacier kept dropping its load and spread the morainal material over the countryside. In some places this moraine is more than 150 metres (500 feet) deep and completely hides the old preglacial surface. This region is now one of America's most productive agricultural areas.

WHAT'S COLD, BLACK, WET AND SLIMY AND EATS SHOES?

A bog. A bog is the same as a swamp. If you were to step into one, your feet would sink down into the mud and water would gurgle up over the tops of your shoes. In Alaska, stunted 100-year-old spruce and fir trees grow in these types of swamps. They are so small because growing conditions are so harsh. If you were to go walking in this swamp, go in winter—at this time the swamp is frozen solid.

A BOG WITH SIGNPOSTS ...

This is Viru Raba, in Estonia ('Raba' is Estonian for bog). It was formed when a glacial moraine dammed a small river at this point. As the moraine is well-drained and made of sand and soil, large trees grow along it. Behind the moraine is a huge bog.

... AND A BOARDWALK TOO!

A boardwalk made of floating wooden planks has been built into the bog. This makes it possible for you to walk about 4 kilometres (2½ miles) into the centre of the bog. If you did, you would notice how flat the land is, like the swamps in Alaska. The large European Glacier, as it melted about 10,000 years ago, made the moraine that dams the bog.

A RESTAURANT FOR STORKS

In summer, this area provides storks and other birds with a smorgasbord of food. Millions of mosquitoes, flies and other insects live in the bog along with frogs and fish. Swamp grasses, flowers and shrubs provide nectar and seeds for birds. In winter, when food is scarce, the birds fly out to warmer climates.

THE PLANTS AND ANIMALS MOVE

STRENGTHS AND WEAKNESSES

Deciduous trees, those that drop their leaves in autumn and winter, require at least 4 months with summer temperatures above 10°C (50°F). When this and other climatic conditions are met, deciduous trees are stronger than conifers and will gradually kill them out. Conifers are trees that hold their seed in cones such as pine, fir and spruce and can survive with as little as 1 month of summer temperatures above 10°C (50°F). For this reason coniferous forests are found on the cold side of deciduous forests.

Tundra grasses and shrubs are even hardier. They can grow where average summer temperatures don't even get to 10°C (50°F), but summers are still warm enough for winter snow to melt. Tundras are found on the cold side of coniferous forests.

BEFORE THE LAST ICE AGE

Before the last ice age, the vegetation in North America and Europe was much the same as it is today. Large trees grew in forests and prairie-type grasses grew in some drier zones. In the far northern colder areas, tundra grasses and hardy shrubs survived.

MIGRATING TREES?

As the ice age began, gradually the trees in the northern hemisphere moved south into warmer areas. On the northern edge of the deciduous forests the trees died because the summers were too short and in their place grew conifers. But the conifers in the north died also because it was too cold for them, so tundra plants grew to take their place. You can guess what was happening to the tundra. The northern parts died and were covered by glaciers while the southern tundra plants moved into the area vacated by the conifers. This process was repeated many times until temperatures stopped falling and the trees stopped moving.

PLANTS' LITTLE HELPERS: BIRDS AND ANIMALS

Birds and animals that eat fruit and seeds spread plants into new areas. Some plant seeds have sharp hooks that catch onto animal fur or bird feathers and are carried by their hosts to other places. Other seeds are hard to digest and may pass through the animal's stomach to end up in their manure. Even squirrels that collect and bury acorns sometimes forget where they buried their winter food supply. Forgotten acorns sprout to grow into large oak trees.

BIRDS, ANIMALS AND INSECTS ALSO HAD TO MIGRATE.

Birds, animals and insects live where their food is found. As plants provide much of their food, the birds, animals and insects are forced to move in step with the trees, shrubs and grasses. But if you have legs or wings it much easier to move than if you are held to the ground by roots, isn't it?

THE BIG HUMAN MIGRATIONS

LAND BRIDGES

On page 16 you read that sea level dropped by 130 metres (425 feet) during the last ice age. This meant that islands now separated from continents by shallow seas were, during the ice ages, joined to those continents by solid land. We call these now drowned land connections land bridges. Land bridges joined Russia to Alaska and New Guinea to Australia.

The last ice age and its ending gave the world its greatest ever human migrations. People spread out of the Mediterranean area, the Middle-East, India and East Asia to populate Australia, both North and South America, and northern and middle Europe.

AUSTRALIAN ABORIGINES MADE THE FIRST MOVE

About 50,000 years ago people from southern India travelled by land bridge to be the very first humans to live in Australia. The land bridge wasn't complete. There were still some deep-water channels to cross on the way. It was not possible to see land on the other side of the channels and these fearless explorers and travellers crossed using simple boats and rafts. The Aborigines settled Australia and continued by land bridge to settle Tasmania.

THEN CAME THE INDIGENOUS AMERICANS

The Indigenous Americans crossed from East Asia to Alaska on dry land. They could not, however, move into the remainder of North America because glaciers blocked their way. It was only after the glaciers began to melt that they were able to proceed further. The background picture opposite is of Cliff Palace in Mesa Verde National Park, Colorado in the USA. The people who lived here were indigenous Americans. Once into North America they quickly spread right down to the southern tip of South America. The last people to cross the land bridge before it was flooded again were the Inuit. The Inuit people are sometimes called Eskimos.

AND FINALLY THE SCANDINAVIANS

The last area of Europe to be settled was Scandinavia, the area that now contains the countries of Norway, Finland and Sweden. It took at least another 2000 years after Western Europe was fully settled before the ice finally melted in Scandinavia. Much of the surface was left rocky and bare so that it took several more thousand years before the forests grew and it became suitable for humans.

WHO OR WHAT KILLED THEM?

Some animal species died out during and at the end of the ice age. These include mammoths and cave bears in Europe, Sabre Tooth Tigers in North America and giant marsupials in Australia. Their extinction coincided with the arrival of humans. For this reason some scientists believe that the newly arrived humans hunted them to extinction. Other scientists are of the opinion that these animals died out because they could not adapt quickly enough to suit the new climatic conditions. Today's scientists are worried that another wave of extinctions could occur if climate warming continues.

VALLEY GLACIERS

Valley or alpine glaciers are common in the high mountain areas of Europe, North America, South America and New Zealand. There are even some close to the equator such as on Mt Kilimanjaro in Tanzania and Mt Kenya in Kenya. Even though there are many valley glaciers, they account for only a small volume of the Earth's glacial ice, less than 1 per cent.

MANY HAVE TRIBUTARY GLACIERS

During the ice ages the valley glaciers grew to be much longer and thicker than the ones now in the world. Some exceeded 100 kilometres (60 miles) in length and most had tributary glaciers in the same manner as large rivers have tributaries.

VERY DIFFERENT TO CONTINENTAL GLACIERS

Alpine glaciers make the region in which they are found more mountainous than they were before the ice age started. This occurs because the alpine glaciers erode their valleys to be much deeper than before the ice age, but leave many of the peaks still standing at their previous height. This is quite different to the action of continental glaciers that tend to smooth off the landscape, leaving it flat.

POSTCARD SCENERY

Glaciated valleys have a special shape. Valleys cut by rivers have a 'V' shape, but those cut by glaciers have a 'U' shape. Was this valley shaped by a glacier or river? Yes, it was shaped by a glacier.

A HANGING VALLEY?

Notice the waterfall in this photo. The bottom of the 'U' shaped Yosemite Valley in the USA used to be up level with the top of that waterfall before the ice ages began. During the ice age a glacier slowly ground its way down the valley lowering the valley floor by more than 500 metres (1,650 feet). When the climate warmed the glacier retreated and melted away leaving the original river tributary 'hanging' on the valley side. To join the main river the tributary now flows over a high waterfall to tumble into the valley below. The waterfall is called Bridal Veil Falls. Can you guess why?

HIGH UP IN THE MOUNTAINS

Valley glaciers start in cirques, sheltered gullies high in the mountains. (Cirque is a French word pronounced 'sirk'.) Snow collects in these cirques and if enough falls it compresses into ice and starts sliding downhill. Only after it starts to move is it classified as a glacier. At the end of the ice age many valley glaciers melted away and the cirques now look like giant armchairs with steep backs and sides and open to the front.

SHARP PEAKS

Mountain peaks, if carved back by cirques on three or more sides, develop sharply pointed tops. The steep faces of the Matterhorn in Switzerland are the backs of cirques that developed on three sides of this mountain peak. Sharp pointed mountains are called horns because people imagine that they look likes the horns on a bull. The Matterhorn is in the German speaking part of Switzerland where 'matter' is the German word for mother. So what does Matterhorn mean?

DOWN IN THE VALLEY

WHAT'S IN A NAME?

Glaciologists, scientists who study glaciers, call the material carried under or on a glacier, moraine. They also use the same term to name this material after it has been dropped on the ground. So, when talking about moraines we usually add another word such as lateral (side), medial (middle), terminal (end), recessional (retreating), or ground (spread widely) before the word 'moraine'. The moraine pictured here is a lateral moraine.

MEDIAL MORAINES

If a tributary glacier carrying lateral moraines joins a main glacier that also has lateral moraines, the two middle ones will form a single moraine away from the sides. Moraines formed in this manner are termed medial moraines and once formed they don't get any larger. Can you work out why? Yes, that's right. Because rocks further down the valley will fall onto the edges of the glacier, not out in the middle. The more tributaries a main glacier has, the more medial moraines it will have on its surface. How many medial moraines can you see on this glacier?

DOING THE JOB OF 1000 DUMP TRUCKS

As an alpine glacier moves down valley it erodes huge quantities of rock, gravel and sand that it carries along under the ice in the same way as a continental glacier (see page 19). But, unlike the continental glaciers, it also collects large amounts of rocky material on its top and sides.

LATERAL MORAINES

Lateral moraines are the ones that develop along the sides of a glacier. Avalanches and rockslides that start high above the glacier tumble down hill to fall onto the glacier's surface. The glacier then carries this material all the way down to its end where it drops it as the glacier melts

WHAT HAPPENS TO THESE LATERAL AND MEDIAL MORAINES?

When the glaciers eventually melt the lateral moraines may remain as long, rocky ridges along the edge of the valley. But you don't find the remnants of medial moraines very often as water from the melting glacier washes them away.

TERMINAL AND RECESSIONAL MORAINES.

When a valley glacier reaches its furthest point down-valley it dumps the material carried under and on it forming huge ridges of piled rock and sand that run across the snout of the glacier. These ridges are called terminal, or end moraines. This is exactly the same as continental glaciers. If temperatures rise the snout melts back up the valley to a point where again its rate of forward motion is equal to the rate of melting. At this point the melting glacier will form another cross-valley ridge that we call a recessional moraine. Recessional means going back.

GROUND MORAINE

In between terminal and recessional moraines a retreating glacier will drop some of its moraine haphazardly on the valley floor. This is called ground moraine. This rough ground moraine was dropped by a retreating glacier in the French Alps.

WHERE GLACIERS MEET THE SEA

STILL BEING MADE IN SOME PLACES

Fjords (pronounced 'fee-ords') are spectacular U-shaped valleys that run into the sea. Both valley and continental glaciers can form them. They can be described as drowned glacial valleys. Fjords are still being formed in those parts of the Earth that are still in an ice age; Antarctica, parts of the Arctic Islands including Greenland, Iceland and Baffin Island.

CLEAR, DEEP WATER

The European Glacier slid off the Norwegian Mountains straight into deep ocean water. River valleys that existed before the ice age became spillways for the huge and spreading glacier. Tongues of glacial ice slid down these valleys deepening them by more than 500 metres (1650 feet) and giving them their U shape. During the coldest period when sea levels were 130 metres (425 feet) lower than now, the glaciers slid out into the ocean.

DEEP RIGHT UP TO THE EDGE

As sea level rose at the end of the ice age water flooded back into the fjords drowning the valleys and rising partway up the cliffs. If you are fortunate enough to cruise the fjords in spring you will see water from the melting snow cascading over towering cliffs and drenching you with spray as it falls into the water beside you.

DRIVE CAREFULLY
Between the scoured plateau above, and the fjord waters below, are cliffs, waterfalls and very steep roads.

JUST THE SPOT FOR A PICNIC
This is as far north as you can go in Europe. Between the ends of these headlands and the North Pole there is nothing but water and sea ice. If you kept going in that direction you would end up in Alaska. Even though the ice age has ended here it's still too cold for trees to grow.

WHAT? A FLOATING GLACIER
When glaciers reach the sea they push out into the water. If the water is deep the snout begins to float because ice is less dense (lighter) than water. Pieces of the glacier will then break off and float away as icebergs. These small icebergs are in Antarctic waters.

AUSTRALIAN AND NEW ZEALAND GLACIERS

ICING ON THE CAKE

At the ice age's coldest, the Kosciuszko (Australian) ice sheet was continuous, but only covered 15 to 20 square kilometres (6 to 8 square miles). Although it was a continental glacier it behaved more like a cluster of smaller glaciers each spilling over the edge of the plateau and quickly melting. From above it would have looked like icing dribbling over the edge of a cake. Ice depths probably did not exceed 200 metres (660 feet). Now that the glacier has gone the area looks just like similar highland areas in Norway and Canada.

NEW ZEALAND'S GLACIERS

New Zealand still has valley glaciers, most of them on the western side of the South Island. The Fox Glacier flows from Mt Cook, the country's highest Mountain, down nearly to sea level. This makes it easy to reach and trained guides are available to lead visitors over its frozen surface. During the Ice Ages glaciers on the western side of Mt Cook reached down and into the sea carving fjords to equal the beauty of those in Norway.

The ice ages had very little effect in the Southern Hemisphere other than for the Antarctic continent. Nearly all of Australia, Africa and South America lie further from the poles than does Europe and parts of Asia and North America. For this reason they did not experience the extreme cold of the ice age northern hemisphere.

DIRTY GLACIERS

Due to the nature of the rock that the Tasman Glacier passes through its surface is almost completely covered by rocks that have fallen onto it from the valley sides. If that's the amount of moraine carried on the glacier's surface, just think how much it carries underneath.

The Tasman Glacier finishes in a pool of water around 100 metres (330 feet) deep. You can only see 10% of the glacier in this photo; the other 90 per cent lies below water level. Rocks from the melting glacier almost fill the hole and will continue to fill the hole as the glacier retreats with global warming.

COLOURED FROM AUSTRALIA

The black marks on this New Zealand glacier are caused by ash from wild fires burning in Australia. The ash has been blown 2 000 kilometres (1 250 miles) by strong westerly winds.

GLACIER'S VERSION OF A WATERFALL

The New Zealand glacier in the background photo opposite is plunging over a very steep slope in its bed. If the glacier melts due to global warming a waterfall will form here.

ACTIVITIES

QUIZ

1. When did the last ice age finish? (page 6)

2. Find three reasons for Antarctica being very cold. (page 14)

3. Which city or town closest to you would be affected by any increase in sea level caused by global warming? What would the effect be?

4. Why, during the ice ages, were Indigenous Australians able to walk from Victoria to Tasmania without getting their feet wet? (page 16)

5. What are the main differences between continental glaciers and valley glaciers? (page 19)

6. Why can't a glacier's crevasses be deeper than 100 metres (300 feet)? (page 21)

7. Why did Indigenous people arrive in Australia before the American Indians reached North America? (pages 34–35)

8. How do icebergs form? (page 41)

THINGS TO DO

Using two colours of plasticine, make a model of a valley containing a glacier showing a glacial horn, a U shaped valley and a cirque. You might even put some sand under the glacier to make it more realistic. Make the glacier so that it can be lifted out of its valley. After the glacier has been removed, use a third colour of plasticine to add to model 1 an end moraine, some ground moraine, a recessional moraine and two lateral moraines.

Write a story from the point of view of the first humans to cross the land bridge from Asia to Australia or from Asia into North America.

Look at the coastlines of western Norway, or southern Chile, or the west coast of the South Island of New Zealand in an Atlas. All those long, thin bays are fjords. Make a freehand drawing of one of these sections of coast.

WANT TO KNOW MORE?

BOOKS

Breidahl, H (2002), Pleistocene Times, Macmillan, South Yarra, Australia.

Donnelly, K (2003), Ice Ages of the Past and the Future, Powerkids Press, New York, USA.

Jay, M (2003), Ice Age Beasts, Chrysalis Children's Books, London, England.

Kirkwood, Roger (2008), Antarctica, New Holland, Sydney, Australia.

Knapp, B (1992) Glacier, Atlantic Europe, Reading, England.

Morrissey, D (1995), The Ice Age, Macmillan, South Melbourne, Australia.

Riley, P (2007), Survivor's Science in the Polar Regions, Wayland, Lewes, England.

Seymour, S (1987), Icebergs and Glaciers, Morrow, New York, USA.

Teitelbaum, M (2002), Chills, Thrills and Spills: Sid's Subzero Survival Skills, Harper, New York.

Walker, S (1990), Glaciers: Ice on the Move, Carolrhoda Books, Minneapolis, U.S.A.

WEBSITES

www.coolantarctica.com/ This site provides information on Antarctica. On the home page, click 'facts' or 'history'.

www.classroom.antarctica.gov.au A children's site for information on Antarctica.

www.athropolis.com/links/glacier.htm This easy-to-use site features a wide range of information on glaciers.

GLOSSARY

ALPINE GLACIER	A glacier located within a river valley or sheltered mountain gully.
AXIS	See earth axis.
ADVANCE	The forward movement of the front of a glacier.
BOG	See swamp.
CIRQUE	The place where an alpine glacier starts. After a glacier has melted it may contain a lake.
CLIMATE	Average weather conditions including temperature and precipitation.
CONIFER	Trees and shrubs that bear their seeds in a cone. The most common are: fir, spruce, hemlock and pine trees.
CONIFEROUS FOREST	A forest of conifer trees.
CONTINENTAL GLACIER	An extremely large glacier that is large enough to fill valleys and cover most mountains.
CREVASSE	A deep crack in glacial ice.
DECIDUOUS	Trees and shrubs that lose their leaves in winter. The most common are: poplar, oak, maple, aspen, birch, ash and elm.
EARTH AXIS	The centre line from the north pole to the south pole around which the earth revolves.
EARTH ORBIT	The path the earth follows as it circles the sun.
END MORAINE	A ridge of rock and sand which forms across the snout of a glacier.
EQUILIBRIUM	A point of balance. When applied to a glacier it occurs when the rate at which the glacier's snout melts back is equal to the speed of its forward movement.
ERODE	To wear away.
ERRATIC	A rock transported by a glacier and then dropped in a place away from where it originated.
EVAPORATE	The change of liquid water into an invisible gas called water vapour.
EXPAND	To grow larger.
EXTINCTION	The killing out of animals or plants to a point where they no longer exist on Earth.
EXTRUSION	When applied to glaciers, refers to the outward spread of a continental glacier caused by pressure from a build up of snow at the glacier's centre.
FJORD	A glacial valley flooded by the sea.
GLACIALS	The cold periods within a series of ice ages.
GLACIER	A body of moving ice or ice that shows evidence of movement sometime in the past.
GLACIOLOGIST	A scientist who studies glaciers.
GLOBAL WARMING	A consistent gradual increase in world temperatures.
GROUND MORAINE	Rocky and sandy material dropped haphazardly on the ground as the glacier retreats.
HANGING VALLEY	A tributary valley left perched high on the side of a main valley that has been deepened by glacial erosion.
ICE AGE	A period in time when the Earth's temperatures were 4 to 8°C colder than they are

presently.

ICEBERG
A portion of a glacier that has broken free and fallen into the ocean, or a section of sea ice that has broken and floated away from an ice shelf.

ICE SHELF
Permanently frozen ocean surface that is attached to land along at least one its sides.

INDIGENOUS
Native, original or the first.

INTERGLACIAL
Warmer periods that lie between ice ages.

LAND BRIDGE
Exposed land that joined one island to another when ice age sea levels were lower than at present.

LATERAL MORAINE
Rock, sand and other debris that has fallen onto a valley glacier's edge and is carried along by the glacier. It is also the name given to the same material after the glacier has deposited it as it melts.

MEDIAL MORAINE
A moraine formed by the joining together of two lateral moraines. It is also the name given to the same material after the glacier has deposited it as it melts.

MIGRATE
To move or change location.

MORAINE
Rock, sand and other material carried on or under a glacier as it moves. It is also the name given to the same material after the glacier has deposited it as it melts.

ORBIT
See Earth orbit.

PENINSULA
A long thin finger of land jutting into the sea from another larger body of land such as a continent.

PLEISTOCENE
The time period from the beginning of the last series of ice ages, through to the end of the last ice age. From about two million years ago through to about 12 000 years ago.

PRAIRIE
A natural grassland found where occasional severe droughts make it difficult for trees to grow.

PRECIPITATION
Rain, hail, snow and dew, which falls to the ground from out of the atmosphere.

RASP
A carpenter's tool, somewhat like a file, with many large teeth.

RETREAT
The backward melting of a glacier's snout.

SCOUR PLAIN
A rocky surface left smoothed over by a continental glacier.

SEA ICE
The frozen surface of a sea or ocean.

SEA LEVEL
The line that marks where the land and sea water meet.

SNOUT
The front of a glacier.

SWAMP
A flat, poorly drained, permanently wet area of land; a bog.

TERMINAL MORAINE
A ridge of rock and sand that forms across the snout of a glacier.

TERMINUS
The end or snout of a glacier.

TREE LINE
A line marking the point where it becomes too cold for trees to grow.

TRIBUTARY GLACIER
A smaller glacier that joins into a larger glacier.

TRIBUTARY RIVER
A smaller river that runs into another larger river.

TROPICS
That area of the Earth that lies between the Tropic of Cancer and the Tropic of Capricorn. 23.5° north and south of the Equator.

TUNDRA
Low shrubs and other plants that grow in areas too cold for other plants.

VALLEY GLACIER
See alpine glacier

VEGETATION
Plants such as trees, shrubs, grasses and ferns that grow on the Earth's surface.

WATER CYCLE
The never ending movement of water in its liquid, solid and gaseous forms through the atmosphere, on land and in rivers, lakes and oceans.

INDEX